KENYA'S NOMADS

An AMECUS STREET Book

KENYA'S NOMADS

Photos and text
by B. C. Ross-Larson

Edited by Paul J. Deegan

An AMECUS STREET Book

An Imprint of
CREATIVE EDUCATIONAL SOCIETY, INC.
MANKATO, MINNESOTA

PUBLISHED BY AMĒCUS STREET, INC.
515 North Front Street, Mankato, Minnesota 56001

Library of Congress Number: 71-190187
Standard Book Number: 87191-209-0

Printed in the United States of America

Designed by Paul J. Deegan

Keeping a cow fed and watered is the most important thing in the lives of some of the world's people. Caring for cattle is the basis of their way of life. One group of people who live this way are the Samburu (Sahm-boo-roo) tribesmen of northern Kenya.

Some 50,000 Samburu live in this East African nation. Their home is about 10,000 square miles of plateau and dry lowlands. They live off their herds of cattle, goats, and sheep.

There are no actual boundaries of the Samburu area because the area is shared with other tribes. Battles between tribes determined the general boundaries now observed. The fighting established the right of a tribe to use a particular region.

The British, who governed Kenya from the 1890's until 1963, tried for many years to establish specific boundaries for the Samburu. But their efforts were not completely successful. The Samburu were generally unwilling to abandon or change their traditional ways.

However, the arrival of the British in Kenya was fortunate for the Samburu. During the 1880's, the Samburu cattle were almost wiped out by disease. The Samburu themselves were scattered among neighboring tribes. Here they first came into contact with Europeans. The Samburu were given assistance by an allied tribe in rebuilding their herds. The Samburu also concentrated on breeding their sheep and goats so these animals could be exchanged for the more valuable cattle.

Ten years or so after the cattle had been nearly destroyed, a smallpox epidemic struck the Samburu. As a result, some enemy tribes were able to successfully raid the Samburu. The raiders took over the country that had long belonged to the Samburu. British soldiers helped protect the Samburu and halted tribal warfare in the region. The British Colonial Office exercised some measure of control over the Samburu for many years thereafter. The Northern Frontier District, which includes the Samburu territory, was created in 1910. Maralal (MAR-ah-lahl) was established as a colonial outpost.

Today it is the major trading center in Samburu country. The
British tried to introduce modern methods of herding cattle.
But the Samburu never really cooperated. Even today the
Samburu are not eager to recognize the authority of the Kenya
government. Kenya has been governed by Africans since it
obtained its independence from Great Britain in 1963. The

SAMBURU COUNTRY

░░░ Samburu Country

Samburu withdrew from participation in one of Kenya's
original two major political parties before the nation's first
government was formed. That party later folded.

The Samburu are represented in the present national
government. The Samburu home area is administered by a
county council. The Samburu tribesmen, however, have neither
the time nor the interest needed to participate effectively in
government. They prefer to handle political affairs in
their traditional manner.

The land where the Samburu live is considered by them to
belong to the tribe, not to any individual or group. There

is no personal ownership of land as we know it in Western
society. The countryside, where Samburu cattle graze, is wild
and unfenced. The Samburu territory is mostly semi-desert. The
annual rainfall of 10 to 20 inches is unpredictable. Rain often
comes in downpours and topsoil is continually being eroded.
Drought is frequent. Living conditions are hard. A
small highland plateau affords better conditions. But its size
limits its use. Most Samburu live in the lowlands.

It would be very difficult to raise crops in this dry
region. But cattle can not only survive, they usually grow to
maturity. The cattle and smaller livestock provide the Samburu
with a way of life. A life style dependent upon raising
cattle in open country is called pastoralism. The word is taken
from the Latin word for shepherd. The Samburu are nomads.
This means that they have no permanent residence — no
one place they call home. They move with their livestock to new
areas when fresh grass and more water are needed. This
movement from place to place on a somewhat regular basis
is known as migration.

A group of Samburu families will stay in one place as long
as there is sufficient water and grazing land for their cattle.
A settlement will migrate on the average of once every
five weeks. The size of a settlement will range from five to
fifteen families. The number will vary depending upon the

amount of water and grass available and the distance between settlements. Other factors also influence the size, location, and duration of Samburu settlements. These include the weather, the location of other tribes, and the presence or absence of predators — animals that attack the livestock.

Settlements must be large enough to supply the labor force necessary to manage and protect the herds. Yet settlements must remain small enough to avoid serious competition among their livestock for water and food.

A settlement usually consists of five to twenty huts arranged in an oval pattern. Since the Samburu practice polygamy (pah-LIG-ah-me, a man may have more than one wife), each married woman lives in her own hut. A man will have a hut for his other wives — if he has more than one. Not all Samburi men marry another wife. It is not always possible to support two or more wives and their children.

When settlements migrate, families often move independently. A particular family may or may not remain with the settlement when it relocates. Any senior male of a Samburu family may approach a settlement new to him and request that he be permitted to live there. If he asks politely, he will always be accepted — even if a particular settlement's resources are limited. This type of conduct both results from and strengthens tribal unity. The Samburu are very dependent upon one another. Should one man suffer misfortune with his livestock, more fortunate friends will grant his request for a few animals with which to rebuild his herd. He may very well be asked to repay the favor in the future.

The settlements offer protection to the member families and
provide a large labor force to care for the cattle. Wild
animals such as lions and elephants sometimes threaten Samburu
herds. Other tribes or rival clans might also try to rustle a
settlement's cattle. All the men in the settlement cooperate to
protect each family's herds. Occasionally a stock owner
might have to rely on the other men in a settlement for help
in caring for his herd. A stock owner is the senior male
member of a family group. Some stock owners are not always
able to properly manage their herds, even with the help
of their sons.

Each settlement is encircled by a six-to-eight-feet high fence
of branches. The fence keeps in cattle and, hopefully, keeps
predators and rustlers out. An opening in the fence is
known as the gateway. The animals are driven through it each
morning to be watered and grazed. After they return through it
in the evening, the gateway will be closed for the night.
Within the settlement, a network of branch fences form corrals
for family herds. These corrals are usually joined by gates.

Occasionally a settlement may remain in one location for
years. But this is rare though the Samburu migrate not
by choice, but by necessity. The region's natural resources and
the Samburu's use of these resources require frequent movement.
Migration tires the people and can weaken livestock, but it is
an essential part of Samburu life. The cattle must have
food and water.

Samburu cattle are called Boran, a type of cattle native
to East Africa. The Boran appear scrawny. They
give less milk than more carefully bred cattle does in
the United States. But they provide enough milk for the
Samburu to live. Milk makes up the major part of the Samburu
diet. A goat or sheep is usually slaughtered for meat only
during the dry season when there is not enough milk. A cow
will be killed for meat only for a ceremonial occasion or in
very bad times. However, if a cow dies, it will be eaten.
Hopefully for a herdsman, this will not happen often. And it
usually doesn't because the Boran are very hardy. Through
the years they have acquired a resistance to many diseases.
Despite the far from ideal conditions under which they're raised,
Boran cattle generally survive. But their environment is still
their greatest threat. Many more cattle die from lack of water,
insufficient food, and disease than are killed by predators
or stolen by rustlers.

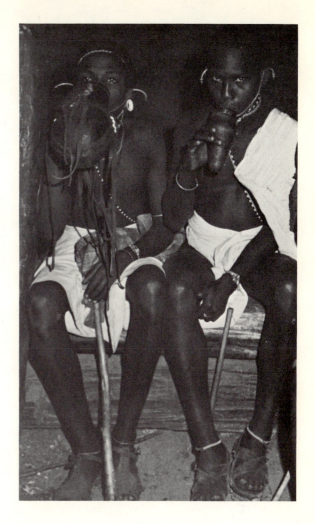

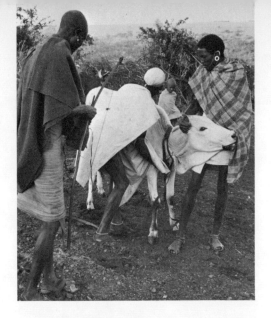

During an extended dry spell, milk is scarce. The cow's production is reduced because they don't have enough water or food. If things get really tough for the Samburu, they may take blood from a bull for food. The blood is rich in protein. A young bull is usually selected. The animal is first separated from a herd. One warrior then holds the bull while another tightens a noose around the animal's neck. This causes the bull's jugular vein to stick out. An older man then tests the vein for pressure before its outer layer is pierced by a short-tipped arrow shot from a bow. About one quart of the animal's blood is collected (photo below). The noose is then released and the wound clots naturally, halting the flow of blood. The bull is kept near the settlement for a day or so until it recovers from the loss of blood.

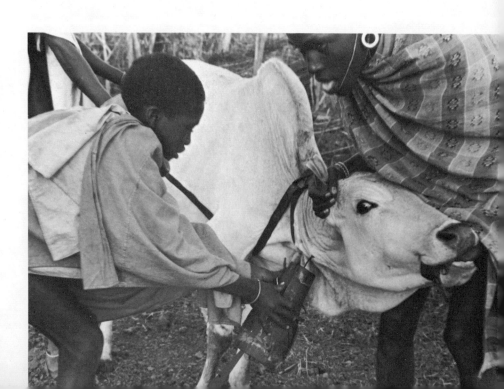

The strong family relationships found among the Samburu benefit them during draught or other trying times. Kinship ties are very evident in Samburu settlements. The family units making up a settlement are often closely related to the senior stock owner in the group. His sons frequently stay with the father's settlement even after they marry. The sons work to increase their own herds before setting out on their own. If a Samburu woman's husband dies, she will not remarry. She will

usually remain with the settlement in which her husband
was living.

Clan relationships are also reflected in the makeup of
settlements. A clan is a social unit broader than a family. It
is based on descent from a common ancestor. Even clan members
who live far apart will often keep in contact.

The most important persons in the settlement — and in
Samburu society — are the elders. An elder is an adult Samburu
man who owns livestock. A man becomes an elder when he
is between 30 and 35 years of age, shortly after he marries.
About 20 years later, he will become a senior elder. Most
societies which do not emphasize formal education and do not
have organized economic systems value highly the judgments

of older persons. They have experienced many things; therefore they are expected to be capable of making wise decisions.
The elders govern Samburu life. Women, warriors, and children do not participate in decision making although they do most of the work in caring for the herds and keeping up the settlements.

Elders carry staffs and wrap large cloths or blankets around their shoulders. These garments fall to the knee. They cut their hair short in contrast with the long braids worn by young men. The elders wear a simple brass earring instead of the round ivory ear plugs used by warriors.

Decisions involving settlement activities or the solution of disputes between people are made in meetings or discussions of the elders.

Elders must select the location of a settlement. It is easier to take care of cattle in open country than in bush areas. But the food is often sparse in open country, while there is usually ample grazing in the bush. But herding is more difficult in the bush. Stray cattle are likely to be lost. The location of natural salt deposits is also a factor in determining where to settle. Many animals, including cattle, must have salt in their diet. If there are natural deposits in the area, cattle will be driven to them while they're grazing. Otherwise, salt must be provided by the stock owner. Calves and goats are given salt in troughs at the settlement.

Elders must choose which factors are most important for the herd at a given time. Once stock owners have become familiar with certain areas, they are likely to remain within the area whenever possible. Severe drought, however, would force them to migrate into unfamiliar territory.

The elders must also decide when it's time to migrate. They make daily decisions concerning the watering of animals and the grazing of cattle. Marriage partners for younger Samburu are agreed upon by the elders. The age at which warriors become elders is established by the elders. This is an important control in a society based upon the relationship of age groups, a society ruled by the old. The elders also control the ceremonies which warriors must pass through to become elders. The warriors — teenage boys and men under 30 — are of course, physically, the strongest members of Samburu society. But they are kept in check. The elders prolong their positions of authority by keeping young men in the warrior class for many years. The warriors are often displeased with their position. They submit to the elders because of tradition but also because the Samburu believe in the power of the curse — calling misfortune upon someone. If the elders' decisions are challenged or their authority threatened, they will call down

a curse. Many outsiders would consider the curse mere
superstition. But misfortune occurs with great regularity in
the life of the Samburu. And it's often attributed to the curse
of another person. So the elders' wishes are followed in
order to avoid personal misfortune in the future.

Elders might go out with their sons to make sure that the
herds are receiving proper care or to see that water rights
are being respected. But as they grow older, elders spend less time
and energy in physical work. They will spend much of their day
in discussion or in leisure. The elders photographed here are
playing a game similar to checkers. The elders are seen as
having achieved positions of authority and honor and are not
expected to work hard. They respond to this status by
being reserved in manner. They can accomplish their goals
without a show of force.

Warriors, however, do resort to violence on occasion. The
elders disapprove such behavior and discourage it as childish and
irresponsible. But the warriors are often in an uncomfortable
position. Not only must they take second place before the
elders, but the warriors' lengthy training is related to preparation
for fighting with other tribes. Yet large-scale tribal warfare is
no longer carried out although many East African tribes still
live in constant tension with each other. Scattered outbreaks of
cattle stealing and personal violence are not uncommon.
But there are no real wars for the warriors to fight.

The role of warriors today is to protect the tribe, the
settlement, and the herd. When warfare between tribes was
prevalent, the warriors were of great importance as fighters. Now
their main job is to take care of the cattle.

The warriors, however, are the most distinctive feature of Samburu society. A boy becomes a warrior about age 15 when he is circumcised. He will remain in this category for over 15 years. During this time he will do much of the hard work and assume the dangerous tasks in the settlement.

He is already used to working. A Samburu boy begins learning how to care for livestock when he's about six years old. Sheep and goats are less important to the Samburu than cattle, so the care of sheep and goats are entrusted to boys. Even a boy of seven, such as the one pictured here, looks forward to becoming a warrior. Now he wears only the belt of beads which had been put round his waist at birth. The

belt is made larger as he grows and will be worn until his
circumcision initiates him into warriorhood. The long stick he
carries is used in herding the sheep and goats. But when
handled like a spear, he can pretend that he's already a warrior.
Boys from 8 to 18 years of age herd cattle. At first, their
fathers go with them to teach them the proper way of handling
livestock. Later they keep the herd together, water it, and
protect it with little help.

Warriors are sometimes called to drive off elephants that are
bothering the herd. An elephant can easily kill a cow or a
man. The warriors run to the herd and chase off the elephants
by throwing rocks. If an elephant charges, the warriors
throw their spears, aiming for the animal's eyes.

Warriors are supposed to act without fear. They spend much of their time in the open country — the bush. Many of their ceremonies take place in the bush, away from the settlement. Warriors carry a spear or two, a sword, and a short club. They take pride in their ability to make it through tough situations. And this becomes important when they go out with a herd away from a settlement.

If all the stock owners in a settlement always kept their herds nearby, there would soon be a shortage of grazing land and water for the cattle. It would be necessary to migrate even more frequently. This is avoided by sometimes splitting a large group of cattle. One group grazes near the settlement each day under the care of young boys. These animals return to the settlement every night. This is the smallest group and consists primarily of milk cows. They provide food for the settlement and the calves, which are always kept at the settlement.

The second group of cattle is taken away from the settlement. Sometimes it might be only 10 miles away; other times it might be 100 miles. Warriors are among those who accompany this group. They establish small camps and sleep in lean-tos. Crude fences of branches are put up each night to enclose the cattle. Life is rough in these camps. Food is sparse. The young men take little with them so that they can move quickly and take advantage of the best grazing possibilities. The cattle are interchanged between the two groups on a regular basis so that all will get an opportunity for better water and grazing.

When the warriors are camping with a herd, they will sometimes slaughter a goat for meat. This is done on a bed of leaves. The animal is carefully skinned because the hide is useful. Warriors eat meat only with each other. Boys who have not been circumcised do not eat with them. Neither boys nor warriors may eat when women are present.

Most of a warrior's activities are shared only with other warriors. Elders determine much of their conduct and many restrictions are placed on their behavior. Even though teenage girls marry, the warriors may not. In fact, they may enter only the huts of their mothers or mothers of other warriors. This custom makes it difficult for them to spend time alone with girls or young women. However, warriors still manage to have girl friends. Eventually, however, a warrior's girl friend will be given as a wife to a much older man. The practice of delaying marriage for young men means that many young women are available for marriage to the elders. Polygamy can be maintained and the elders will therefore continue to have children available to care for their stock. An elder may also be able to increase the numbers of his herd because of the additional help. The number of cattle belonging to a man is the sign of wealth in Samburu society.

The young warrior, however, has a long wait before he can become an important man. Ceremonies celebrate the beginning and end of the two warrior classes — junior and senior. The warriors are aware of their role and take pride in their appearance. They wear beads and chains. Their long hair is braided and their heads and bodies are painted with ocher (OO-ker) — earth with mineral content that provides coloring. The ivory in their pierced ear lobes is carved from cattle horns and elephant tusks. A warrior's main items of clothing is a cloth wrapped tightly around the body. Another light cloth is carried as a protection from the sun, wind, and dust.

When the period to be spent as a senior warrior nears completion, warriors, such as the two pictured on the opposite page, must adopt the ways of elders. Long hair is no longer acceptable. Their conduct must begin to command respect. They must abandon the often carefree and sometimes violent behavior of a warrior.

Even though the Samburu resist change in life styles, some different ways have been accepted. The warriors shown above are visiting young men of their own age who attend school. These students have put aside the garb and weapons of warriorhood. Going to school could eventually lead students to changes in attitudes that will work against Samburu traditions. For the present, however, there is no rivalry between warriors and students. The warriors are proud of the noble life they follow. The students are proud of the education which they believe will give them new opportunities.

There is less opportunity for such pride among Samburu women. They have a position inferior to men. They do not participate in making community decisions. A girl does not participate in the arrangement of her marriage to a man, usually at least twice her age, from another clan. The new wife will go to live with the husband and his relatives, who may live a considerable distance from the area she knows. Samburu wives are expected to have children and are responsible for caring for them. A Samburu mother does not have the labor-saving devices available to many in the United States. Running the household is a fulltime task, leaving very little time for exercising influence on the settlement or tribal communities.

Samburu girls do not pass through the numerous age classifications established for boys. Young girls are expected to shy away from all elders. This means they have very little contact with their own fathers. Girls undergo a ceremony, known as circumcision, in their early teens. Girls who have been circumcised wear goat-skin shirts and cloth wraps. The girls will marry when they are about 17. Then they will be considered women.

Teenage girls receive bead necklaces from their warrior lovers. A girl is proud of the necklaces and wears them for the rest of her life. The number she wears indicates her popularity. Traditional dances provide the opportunity for girls and warriors to meet apart from older persons. The warriors call a dance by banding together outside a settlement. Their deep chanting brings the girls out to join them. The girls pretend they don't really want to go, but one by one they come. They join the repeated jumping and chanting but show little interest in the warriors. Later, one girl will sing a solo to the warriors. Her song first praises them for a daring deed such as rustling cattle or scaring off wild animals. Then she taunts the warriors by calling them cowards. This is done to inspire them in their role as protectors and providers. Following a dance, a girl and young man may pair off, something they would not be able to do within the settlement.

The relationships between a girl and a warrior must always end unfavorably for both since the warrior is not permitted to marry. When he is old enough to marry, his wife will be from another clan and will be much younger. The girls he knows

as a warrior will have been long married to an elder. A
Samburu girl in turn would probably prefer to have a young
warrior for her husband rather than a 35-to-55-year-old elder. But
her father and other male relatives will select her husband. He
will be from another clan because this will strengthen the
family's position by giving it new allies. This is one of the
ways tribal unity is maintained.

The husband will give his wife a certain number of cattle
when they marry. The amount is a matter of serious discussion
between the husband and the girl's male relatives. Some
elders may never be able to arrange for a second wife because
their herd remains small. A stock owner must be rich in
terms of cattle to have a third wife. Although a family's entire
herd is generally kept together, a wife's cattle are considered to
be under her control. This gives her status and influence in
her own household.

Although married women run their households, some of the work expected of them relates to the entire settlement. They milk their own herds each day at sunrise and again in the evening. The milking of the rest of the cattle and goats is also done by women and girls. The milk is collected in a calabash (KAL-ah-bash), a dried, hollow shell of a plant. The milk is often drunk from a cup which also serves as a cup for the calabash. The women are also responsible for supplying the settlement with water. If the water supply is nearby, it is collected each morning in a large calabash. But if the water is several hours walk from the settlement, many calabashes are loaded on donkeys. Enough water is then brought back to last for three or four days.

During their daily work, the women often gather in small groups for conversation. They leave to work at some task, then often return to the conversation. Women do not associate much with elders. They usually stay inside the settlement fence or very close to it. The elders will gather a few hundred yards from the settlement for discussion. Small children can be found near the women. Watching, listening, and later helping their mothers, the girls learn what will be expected of them when they marry. Though only a teenager when married, the Samburu wife has been well prepared in terms of the Samburu tradition for the role of a wife. This is not true of a boy of the same age, who is purposely prepared very slowly for adult responsibilities.

Samburu women make their own clothing and utensils. The shopping trips of a Samburu woman are very different from those of an American housewife. Women transport cattle and goat skins to the Maralal market. The donkey is the Samburu beast of burden. Most homesteads have two or more. At the market, the skins will be traded for maize meal and tea, used at meals during the dry season when the milk supply has run low.

The hut in which a married woman and her children live
is considered part of a woman's household concerns. Building
huts, therefore, is part of a woman's work. So is it taking
it apart, transporting the essential parts, and putting up a new
hut when a settlement migrates. Huts look from the outside
like bread loaves. They are basically rectangles some 15-feet long
and about 10-feet wide. The Samburu who live on the
plateau use thin branches, tied with strips of bark, to support
the ceiling. Walls are lean posts covered with insulating material.
The insulation consists of leaves plastered with a mixture of
mud and dung. There is better grazing land and more water on
the plateau, so migrations don't have to be so frequent as
in the lowland area. The nights are also cooler so the huts
need to provide some warmth. The Samburu living in the
lowland make smaller and more transportable huts. Some lowland
huts are simply hides strung over wooden braces.

A Samburu woman sleeps near the fireplace toward the entrance of a hut. Cooking utensils crowd her bed. The main sleeping area, used by her children, is at the rear of the hut. This area is raised slightly off the floor. Cattle hides, six or seven deep, provide a cushion. Young men usually sleep with their heads on a wooden "pillow" to prevent their carefully braided hair from becoming messed. The huts are small, simple, and lit only by light from a tiny window or flames from the stone fireplace. Sometimes tea and a corn meal are heated over the fireplace to go with the normal milk diet. Money to purchase these food items, tobacco, or other supplies comes from selling livestock at government auctions. This is not done often because the Samburu herdsmen does not raise his cattle to market them — he lives off them.

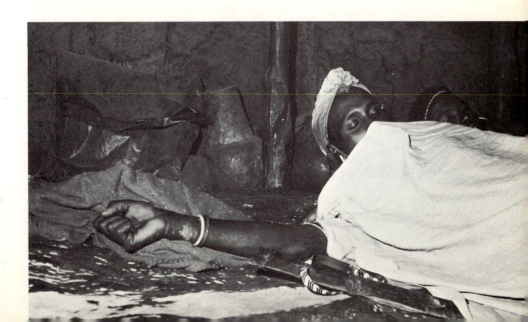

The woman in the photograph below is the first wife of a settlement's major stock owner. Her two warrior sons share her hut. So does her husband. But he will also spend time in the hut of his 16-year-old second wife, shown in the photograph on the opposite page. She doesn't yet have children but visiting friends and close relatives of her husband will use her hut from time to time. Samburu men often leave the settlement where their family is living and visit for a time with relatives or friends in other settlements. This movement of people between settlements strengthens the Samburu tribal relationships.

The woman pictured above is building a hut. While she works, her husband's second wife watches her children. This cooperation among Samburu women in carrying out their daily tasks is common.

Samburu women also participate in their tribe's most essential activity, caring for the livestock, particularly the cattle. The woman in this photograph is giving fodder to calves. This is done to make sure the young cattle get sufficient food. It also accustoms the animals to contact with people. The calves will determine the future success of the herd and they are given special care. Children separate the calves from the herd and the calves are kept near the settlement all day.

The other cattle are taken farther way from the settlement to graze. Elders first instruct the boys and young warriors who will watch the grazing herd during the day. Good planning is necessary to obtain the most food and water from one location, thereby increasing the time the settlement remains in one place.

Watering the livestock is the most critical daily task of Samburu herdsmen. The object is to get the animals watered as quickly as possible. This makes it possible for the cattle to

spend most of the day grazing. Cattle who don't get
enough food will be both leaner and more likely to become
sick. Warriors must learn to establish control over a herd. A
disorderly herd takes longer to water. The photographs on pages
42 and 43 of cattle being watered show a herd that is well
controlled. After drinking in the water hole, the cattle will be
driven to the day's grazing area.

The Samburu must often dig into a dry riverbed to bring
up water. The waterhole dug by the elder in this photograph is
protected by a simple branch fence. Water is scooped from
the hole into a trough made of cowhide. Four or five cattle
at a time are led to the trough. Elders oversee the watering and
do the hard work of scooping the water. They will be able
to relax for the rest of the day. The boys watching the
cattle must not tire themselves early in the day because they
have before them many hours of herding.

Every day the Samburu repeat the routine of watering,
driving the cattle to grazing, herding them all day, and
driving them back to the settlement at sunset for evening milking.
The Samburu give their time and effort to the cattle. In
return, the cattle provide the settlement with milk for food
and hides for clothing, huts, and mattresses. Cattle will usually
be slaughtered for food only when meat is wanted for a
major Samburu ceremony.

Years are needed to build up a large herd. Disease, drought,
predators, or poor management can destroy a herd in months
or even in a few weeks. The size of a Samburu herd varies. A
younger elder may have 50 head of cattle. A senior elder
with good management and some luck may control 250 head.
The average stock owner probably has some 100 head.

The stock owners with large herds are considered the tribe's wealthiest men. In this and in most of its outlook and practices, Samburu society is substantially the same as it was 100, 200, even 300, years ago. The Samburu still cling to a pastoral, nomadic way of life.

The British tried to impose an organized administration upon the Samburu. Some of the practices introduced by the British have been continued. The Samburu must pay taxes. A few roads now break up the landscape in the Samburu district. Health services are provided to tribesmen who will accept them. Kenya's parliament gives the Samburu a voice in matters of government. But few are seriously interested in the world outside their settlement and tribe.

Formal education is also available to young Samburu whose families permit them to attend government schools. This could eventually bring change to the Samburu life style.
Education brings new values and a broader outlook to Samburu children. Some students begin to look outside the tribe for their future. The young man on the opposite page wears Western-style clothing. He speaks English in addition to Samburu — a language similar to that spoken by other pastoral tribes in East Africa. This Samburu sees a choice in a way of life and experiments with the new. He might return to a settlement and follow his father's way of life or he might take up life in a city.

Whatever this young man does, it would seem that it will be a long time before substantial changes occur in the way of life followed by most Samburu. Few are like him: divided between two worlds. Survival is still a daily concern for the majority. Their present way of life meets the most basic needs of their environment. Most Samburu would ask — "Why change?"

BRUCE ROSS-LARSON is
a skilled photographer who has
illustrated several outstanding
books with his sensitive
photographs. His pictures also
have appeared in a number of
exhibits and displays. The
photographs in this book were
taken in 1971 when Ross-Larson
returned to Kenya on
assignment for Amēcus Street.
The 27-year-old Ross-Larson,
a graduate of Yale University,
previously had lived in Kenya
for two years. He has worked
in banking, community relations,
and institutional finance.
Ross-Larson is now living in
Kuala Lumpur where he is
working on a book.